# Kitzoo?! Kitzoo?! Where are you?

Christy Mumma

# Kitzoo?! Kitzoo?! Where are you?

A learning story for children and adults

**TATE PUBLISHING**
AND ENTERPRISES, LLC

Published by Tate Publishing & Enterprises, LLC
127 E. Trade Center Terrace | Mustang, Oklahoma 73064 USA
1.888.361.9473 | www.tatepublishing.com

Tate Publishing is committed to excellence in the publishing industry. The company reflects the philosophy established by the founders, based on Psalm 68:11,
*"The Lord gave the word and great was the company of those who published it."*

Book design copyright © 2014 by Tate Publishing, LLC. All rights reserved.
*Cover design by Allen Jomoc*
*Interior design by Gram Telen*

Published in the United States of America

ISBN: 978-1-63122-206-1
1. Education / Teaching Methods & Materials / General
2. Education / Parent Participation
14.07.18

This is the possible story of a cats' life. It's a very good scenario and the kitten was treated very well, and had a very good home. Not all pets are this lucky. To help prevent suffering, please have your pets' spayed and neutered.

Thank You

# 1

He was born one cold and rainy day in a box made of wood, in an alley way, but, that was okay. It was next to a zoo, this box made of wood. With him were his brothers and sisters and a good, gentle loving mother, to keep him warm, cozy and fed often.

Day turned into night and night turned into day. This went on for a several days.

Next thing he knew, his eyes opened and he could finally see, and feel, his mother and the other kittens. What a sight!

After filling his belly, he could finally watch mother clean the others, one by one, until it was then his turn. It was so comforting having her care for him and give him so much attention! Life is beautiful, how could he be so lucky?

He looked like a tiger, with stripes of orange. But he had a bib of white and four socks to match. And the bib he used, eating a like a tiger. With narrowly pointed eyes and ears up high, he was a very alert and playful kitten. Often, he would try to tackle one of his brothers' then pounce and roll. So much fun!

**Each day, mother would leave and look for food for herself and always come back full and happy.** Being next to a zoo, there was plenty of food. Returning, with a wide smile on her very dignified face, she would then take her place and let the growing kittens eat while she licked her paws clean.

# 2

Then one day, mother left to go for food, as usual, came back full and happy and once again, took her place and, as usual, **let the growing kittens eat**. When they were finally finished, she stood up. Looking down on the kittens, she chose one boy, gently picking him up with her teeth and mouth.

She then walked away with the bundle hanging from her mouth. Upon returning a short time later, his brother was gone! She then, again, gently picked up another and, once again, walked away with another bundle hanging from her mouth, only to return by herself.

This she did again and again, until it was just his sister and he. "What was she doing?" he thought with fear as his eyes grew wide.

Once again she returned, only to next take his sister, and suddenly, he was alone! Alone and scared! **He did not understand his mother had found them a better home, and had to take each kitten, one by one.** With everyone gone, so was the warmth and comfort, and he was starting to shiver. Alone, scared and soooo cold!

Soon, it started getting darker and his mother still hadn't returned. Listening, he could hear the sound of people walking past as they finished work, in their hurried pace, trying to make it home to their families, before darkness fell.

Slowly he peeked out and, out of nowhere, big shoes pounded the pavement and, in an instant, they were gone.

By then, he had quickly backed up into the box and once again, surrounded by the not-so-comforting darkness of where his family had been before mother took each away, one by one.

Not only was he alone, scared and cold, but also hungry now too. His mother did not feed him before leaving with his sister. Before long, for it was feeding time at the zoo, he started having the smells of the feed drifting past his nose.

He tried to breathe in all he could, but it wouldn't make him feel full.

# 3

As the sun fell, he was covered in darkness, except for the strange bright light that lit the streets. By now, he was hungry and starting to get weak because he had no food.

Soon the busy rushing slowed, and all the animals were fed and quietly resting.

He managed to peek out again, just as a big noisy bus pulled up and stopped right in front of him, making him back up quickly, again in fear.

Just then, with banging and clanking sounds, the doors flew open and out came a girl, with a bright and happy smile. As she jumped off the bus, her golden curls bouncing, she went straight to the display windows of the zoo.

In the first window, there were cute little hedgehogs all balled up and sleeping.

Moving to the next window, she saw a small movement in the corner of her eye.

Turning her head, she saw nothing. Thinking she might have imagined it, she turned and looked back into the window. In little dams, made of plastic and steel, were the not-so-busy beavers, trying to sleep off dinner and lazily looking around, as like all the other zoo creatures.

Looking towards the boxes once again, the movement suddenly darted out, then ran into another box behind the dumpster. Quickly and quietly, she tip-toed over to the box and peered inside.

With the street lamps giving some light, she could make out a small form, the color of orange, a fluffy little ball, with huge eyes staring up at her. It was a kitten, cold and scared. "Oh, how sad", she thought.

A cold and scared baby cat, next to the zoo, could this be true? A kitten in front of the zoo, I'll call you Kitzoo!

# 4

Carefully bending over, the girl slowly wrapped her hands around the kitten, scooped him up and wrapped him in her shirt. Finally feeling warmth and comfort, Kitzoo was finally safe! Still shaking, though, not as scared and wrapped in her shirt, all he wanted was food in his belly. Forgetting the chill, filled with sadness and pity, she turned towards her house, in a hurry to feed the kitten.

As she turned the corner, the soft glow of lights she could see coming from the front windows. She hurried and ran up the steps. As the door flew open, it startled everyone inside.

For just a second, they turned and looked, and then returned to their favorite position.

"Mother, Mother, look what I found in front of the zoo! It's a kitten from the zoo, and I named him Kitzoo!" she blurted. As her mother turned and saw the happy, yet sad look in her baby's eye, she could not say no. "I don't like to see you blue, therefore you can keep kitzoo!" she said with an unsure smile.

Peeking out from under the girls' jacket, Oh, what a sight! He saw a warm, blazing fireplace with two figures curled up and sleeping comfortably. The delicious aroma of fresh baked bread in the air, along with many other strange smells, made him more hungry.

Looking around curiously, he also noticed many toys and balls of yarn and warm, soft beds.

This was meant to be home! With anticipation, Kitzoo tried to reach out to get closer to the wonderful smell of the food on the table. It was time to eat!

# 5

As the two of them past the table, sadness overtook Kitzoo, until she took him in the laundry room and closing the door, she placed him on a warm and shaggy carpet.

Reaching over him, she opened a cabinet and pulled out a can. Opening the can, she put the contents on a small plate and placed it in front of kitzoo. Not knowing quite sure what it was that she put down, he moved a little closer.

The smell of the tuna filled his nostrils, once again reminding him of his hunger.

Sticking his nose in the food, he started to eat hastily. Oh, he was so hungry! The food was so good, he never had food like this, and suddenly he forgot about his mother, brothers and sisters, the box he called home, the zoo, all the activity, the cold, and being left alone and scared.

Once licking the plate clean, she gently picked him up and carried him over to the fireplace and put him next to the other two figures, who were both big enough to be mother, but not mother. Barely glancing over, they both continued their purring sleep.

Kitzoo now had a full belly, and a nice warm place to sleep. Slowly his eyes began to close, it was a long day, until, there he was, floating on soft, warm clouds.

In what seemed like minutes, he opened his eyes again and saw it was daylight.

Looking over at the other two as they both stood, stretching one leg at a time, then their whole body, while the sounds of food hit the plates. It was time to eat! Kitzoo jumped up and raced over to the bowls, while the other two sauntered over with content purrs and started eating slowly with pleasure.

Quickly cleaning his bowl, with a very full belly, he went to the next bowl. With a growl and a paw slap, he returned to his bowl. Still no food in the bowl, he cried a sad meow. Unable to say no, the girl poured more food into the dish, which he dove into.

# 6

Finishing the second helping, with his belly too round to move, the others finished, and curiously walked over to the new orange figure. With wonderment, they lowered their noses to take a sniff. Comfortable with what they smelled, they gently started grooming him, one behind his ears and the other on his back.

Oh, how wonderful it felt! It was like his mother all over again, but it wasn't her and no brothers or sisters.

Forgetting his mother, sleeping and playing with his brothers and sisters, the box of wood in the alley way, the comforting sounds of the zoo, being alone and scared, being hungry and cold, forget it all! It was time to explore!

Walking over to the bookshelf, he rubbed up against the books and took a deep breath. With a sneeze, he sent out the dust that he had breathed in. Looking over, he saw a few figurines and danced over, knocking them over, after being placed there with great care.

With a chuckle, the girl picked up the figures and put them back were they belong. Slowly and gently, she put her hand on his head and stroked his back. How lucky could he be?

As the day wore on, sitting in the window with the hot rays of the sun to keep him warm, he was able to look out as people strolled by, talking and laughing. Along the sidewalk, were children, some with toys, some riding small bikes, playing and racing.

Cars drove by with windows open and waving hands. Birds were chirping their songs along with other strange and rude sounds that he later found out were dogs barking. So much activity! He grew tired just watching everything and let out a yawn.

# 7

Taking a cat nap, at the window, he rested peacefully.

Still in a new environment, the thoughts of the day before were starting to disappear. Upon awakening, he stood and stretched, ready to eat again. With no food being out yet, he glanced around and saw the girl as she moved around cleaning, with a sweet sound coming from her mouth. Focusing on the task at hand, for she promised to help clean, she failed to notice the orange ball that hid behind the chair.

Glancing over to the window, where he had been sleeping peacefully, the bed was empty.

"Kitzoo?! Kitzoo?! Where are you?" she sang. Not seeing him, she went back to her tasks. Just as she walked past the chair, he shot out with the intention of tackling her feet, as he had tackled his brothers and sisters, only to slide off her foot and onto the floor. He then heard her scream, with shock and delight, "Oh, Kitzoo! There you are!" she said, and bent over to pick up the bundle.

Soon, once again, it was time to eat. After finishing another great meal, it was time to settle in front of the fire, take a deep breath, and relax. Several content purrs were all that could be heard.

When lights started turning off, feeling more and more at home, Kitzoo jumped up and out of the comfy cat bed and raced into the bedroom. What was happening here? As the girl crawled into bed and opened a book, Kitzoo decided he needed to be up there too.

Looking at the bed, he saw the sheets that were nearly touching the floor.

Trotting over to the bed, he touched the sheet with his foot and it stuck! His nails had stuck into the fabric. Grabbing on with the next foot, and the next, and the next, he found he was able to walk up the side of the bed. This is so great!

Hearing and seeing the form at the bottom of the bed, she smiled as he danced with great care to her hands and book. Allowing him to walk and crawl on her, and with great effort, he was able to climb up to her neck and the soft, golden curls. As she touched his head with her chin, a sweet purring sound started playing from Kitzoo. This is where he would sleep! And she let him.

The next morning as his eyes slowly opened, they suddenly widened in amazement. It was really true! He was not cold and alone! Instead he was wrapped up in a ball, surrounded by the soft, golden curls. When the girl woke, she smiled and picked him up and gently pressed him to her nightgown. Time to eat again!

# 8

As the days turned into night and nights turned into day, Kitzoo grew and grew.

He always had a full belly, a window to watch out, lots of love, a basket full of fun toys, a warm fireplace to sleep by, and a cozy spot to sleep each night. What a life!

Growing up, he had great life and played with her every chance he got. The other two didn't mind, for they were perfectly comfortable, calmly resting. When she sat in the chair, he would jump up in her lap. Whatever she was working on, he also worked on. And so affectionate was he! Even when he was in the way, it was okay.

She always knew where he was, he made it a point. Sliding across the floor, whacking the toy balls, and sending them flying through the air only to bounce off the wall and land noisily back on the floor. At times, she would toss the ball, only to have Kitzoo frantically chase and tackle it.

Other times, he would jump up on the bookshelf and hide next to a book. Trying to remain motionless, and knowing where he was, she would call out for him. "Kitzoo?! Kitzoo?! Where are you?" she would call.

# 9

When reaching his cover, he would fly through the air with his paws outstretched; desperately trying to cling to the first thing a nail could grab. Laughing with delight, her arms wrapping around him, he would hear,

"Oh, Kitzoo! There you are!"

When cooking her meals, while mother was at work, she let him up on the counter and next to the sink while she got the food ready.

Intrigued he was, as she cut, sliced, cooked, stirred and blended. All the while, trying to move closer....and closer....until with a "no" and a gentle push back, forcing him, once again, next to the sink.

This was done again and again. "Oh, Kitzoo! This is not for you!" she replied each time. And Kitzoo thought, each time, "Just a try?"

Each night, as the lights went out; he would follow quietly, waiting for the moment. As soon as she crawled into bed, he would scamper up the bed, wrapping his legs around her neck in a loving hug and giving her a peck on the cheek. He would turn in circles and knead with his feet, up high on her shoulder before finding the perfect spot to curl up and collapse, with a sweet purr in her ear.

# 10

It was a bright and sunny day, on a Sunday it was. The bells chimed letting the townspeople know that mass is soon to begin.

As they always do on Sundays, they got ready for church, in their Sunday best, all prim and proper.

With their hats and jackets, they were ready to go, for the walk to the church, just right around the corner. In a single file they went, with mother in the lead, down the steps they went, to join the others on their way to the service.

Closing the door behind them, or so they thought, the latch slipped off. With the next good breeze, the door suddenly swung open. Staring in amazement, Kitzoo found himself faced with the activity he saw in the window. People returning from an earlier service, with their children running and having fun. Others moved the other way, in a hurry to make it to mass. Big cars with loud honking horns filled the road.

The sounds of people talking and laughing and dogs barking. All the strange sights, he saw from the window, when he took to his pillow, for his afternoon nap.

# 11

Peering over at the other two, who were also looking out, showed no interest in standing, yet alone walking over to the open door. Slowly he crept over to the door, one step at a time. Cautiously, he peeked his head out with his young heart racing. All the sights and new smells!

With great care, he stepped out on the porch and looked around in amazement, in what he saw. Continuing on, he stepped on the grass. Sinking in the thick and soft, green grass, with the fresh smell, he lowered his head and went into a roll. Rolling on his back, he stared into the great blue sky. Lazily, he stretched his legs out as

far as they could go. So much room to move!
"This is amazing", he thought, "How could I be
so lucky?"

Suddenly, he heard a strange rustling sound
coming from behind him, towards the back of
the house. Glancing around quickly, he spied a
flurry of activity in the flower garden. It looked
like a toy, moving by itself! It moved in fast
circles, before shooting towards the fence. What
was this fast new toy, one he never saw before?

# 12

Hopping up in a run, he ran after the toy, he had to have it! Without thinking, he took a final leap, nearly landing on the scared mouse as it rushed through a hole in the fence.

He hit the fence with his head and was still able to reach through the hole with his paw, slapping the mouse's tail. Luckily, the nails missed the tail, as the scared mouse dashed across the next yard and into safety.

With his head starting to throb, he still was so excited! This was still fun!

Still very curious with the new sights around him, he slid along the fence and followed it along the one side of the house. Before long, he found himself in the backyard, which was connected to another yard, which was connected to another yard. Connected they were, by an old wood fence.

The fence was worn with missing boards and chain fence filling the holes. As he climbed onto the porch, he got a better look. So much room!

Jumping off the porch, he sauntered over to the other garden, this one for vegetables. As he walked through the plants, he could smell the delicious aroma of fresh, raw vegetables. He approached a plant with green strings hanging off and bit into one. The flavor filled his mouth. "Mmm!" he thought.

He then walked on and saw plants with red strings hanging, thicker than the green ones. Biting into one, it set his mouth on fire and he turned and ran, trying to outrun the burning, which only got worse.

Finally out of breath, mouth still burning and weak from the run, he stopped and quickly licked his paws, still covered with the taste of the sweet grass. Licking with haste, he could finally see through the tears that formed in his eyes.

With his mouth still burning, though not as bad, he looked around again. What an incredible day!

# 13

Walking over to another fence, he saw the beautiful red flowers. The flowers he often saw in a vase on a table inside. Getting closer, he could smell the familiar scent and quickly rubbed up against the comforting smell. OUCH! Sharp thorns pierced his side, tearing into his skin. **The thorns were always removed inside, this he never knew.**

With the throb in his head, and a mouth still burning, his side was now raw and itchy too.

Starting to get nervous, he realized he was not having fun and just wanted to be back in the safety of home, back to his fun toys, back to the window and the bookshelf, back to helping with dinner, back to the sound of, "Kitzoo?! Kitzoo?! Where are you?"

With the throb in his head and the burn in his mouth and the pain in his side, he started to make his way back to the front porch, from where he had started. He followed the fence along the side of the house, when suddenly; the deafening sounds of the neighbor's three small dogs sent him flying through the air in panic.

Landing on the soft grass, he got his balance and turned quickly in the direction of the offending sounds. Alert and ready to run, he watched as the crazy dogs ripped through the flowers in a desperate attempt, to get through the fence, to the cat next door. They held a terrible grudge to all cats and kittens alike. They wanted nothing more, just to eat, this cat next door. Too terrified to move and his eyes the size of quarters, he prayed to be back home, happy and content.

# 14

For now, his heart ticking faster than a clock, eyes the size of quarters, hair ruffled, head still throbbing, mouth still burning and the pain still in his side, how much worse can it get? Managing to make a mad dash, he made it under the porch, to the safety of the darkness.

The great blue sky, the fresh green grass, the exciting chase of the mouse and all the room to move, no longer mattered. He was scared and alone, also in pain, in the darkness, under the porch.

Hearing the church bells in the air only startled him more. This only made him back up further. Unsure of what to do, he waited. And waited. And waited. There was little light, it felt cold and damp. Once again he prayed to be home…..When suddenly, he heard a sound that was like music to his ears! "Kitzoo?! Kitzoo?! Where are you?"

"Here I am! Here I am!" he tried to say, but out came the sounds of a scared meow. Hearing the cries, the girl raced to the yard and the side to the porch. Bending down and peeking under the porch, she saw, once again, an orange ball, scared and all alone. With a gentle smile and still out of breath, she said, "Oh, Kitzoo, there you are!"

As soon as Kitzoo realized who the shadow was, he raced out from under the porch and jumped up into the warm and gentle hands that he missed so much!

Walking back to the house wrapped in her arms so tight, he heard her say, "Oh, Kitzoo, I thought I lost you!"

The end